All Kinds of

Beliefs

Written by Anita Ganeri

Illustrated by Ayesha Rubio
and Jenny Palmer

FRANKLIN WATTS
LONDON • SYDNEY

First published in Great Britain in 2019
by The Watts Publishing Group
Copyright © The Watts Publishing Group 2019

Designer: Little Red Ant
Editor: Nicola Edwards

HB ISBN: 978 1 4451 6108 2
PB ISBN: 978 1 4451 6109 9

Printed in Dubai

Franklin Watts
An imprint of Hachette Children's Group
Part of The Watts Publishing Group
Carmelite House
50 Victoria Embankment
London EC4Y 0DZ
An Hachette UK Company

www.hachette.co.uk
www.franklinwatts.co.uk

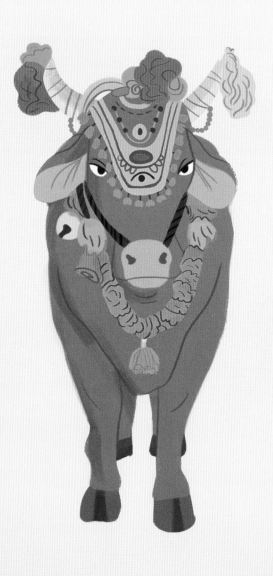

Contents

Children may learn their beliefs from their parents, or from teachers at their school or place of worship.

People's beliefs guide how they live and behave towards others.

Be kind to other people.

Respect your elders.

Treat everyone as equal.

Being part of a religion and having a faith is very important for many people.

Many people believe that there is a God who made everything in the world.

They try to live their lives as God wants them to.

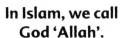

In Islam, we call God 'Allah'.

Christians believe that God sent his son, Jesus, to Earth to help people.

A religion may have many gods or no god.

Hindus believe in a great spirit, called Brahman. There are also many gods and goddesses.

Buddhists don't have a god. We follow the teachings of the Buddha, who lived thousands of years ago.

Some people say prayers as a way of talking to God. They may thank God, ask for help, or tell God how they are feeling.

Some Muslims pray five times every day.

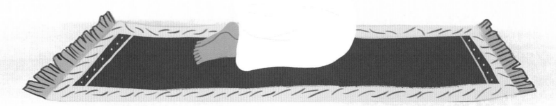

I am a Christian. I say my prayers every night, before I go to sleep.

People's beliefs can affect how and what they eat. Many Hindus do not eat meat because they believe that all life is holy.

After Sikhs worship in a gurdwara, they serve a vegetarian meal, called langar, for everyone to share.

Jewish people avoid eating some foods, such as pork, as part of their religion.

Some people wear special clothes to show their religion. Jewish men and boys wear a small cap called a kippah as a constant reminder of God.

I wear a prayer shawl when I pray.

Sikhs have five signs of their faith, called the Five Ks. One is kesh (uncut hair).

Many religions have special books that are holy to them.

We are learning to read the Qur'an.

Muslims believe that the Qur'an is the word of Allah. They treat this holy book with great respect.

The Christian holy book is the Bible.
Part of it tells the story of Jesus's life.

At Christmas, we listen to the story of Jesus's birth.

My mum reads me a story about Rama and Sita at bedtime.

Hindus have many different holy books. The Ramayana tells stories about the god, Rama, and his wife, Sita.

Religions have special places where people go to meet and worship.

We have a service with hymns, prayers and Bible readings.

Christians worship in a church.

Muslims worship at a mosque.

We hear the call to prayer from a tall tower called a minaret.

This is the Ark where the Torah scrolls are kept. The Torah is our holy book.

Jews worship at a synagogue.

Many Hindus worship at a mandir, or temple. They believe it is God's home on Earth.

We take our shoes off when we go in to show respect.

Inside a Sikh gurdwara is a copy of the Guru Granth Sahib.

The Guru Granth Sahib is our holy book.

We keep the Guru Granth Sahib covered when we are not reading it.

In a vihara, Buddhists make offerings to the Buddha.

We bow and offer flowers, candles and incense.

Many people also worship at home. In most Hindu homes there is a statue or picture of one or more of the gods.

We worship in our prayer room every day.

Shabbat is a day of rest and prayer for Jews. It begins on Friday night, with a special family meal.

Festivals are times when people come together to celebrate. Many festivals remember special events in a religion's history.

At Christmas, Christians celebrate the birth of Jesus.

I love setting up the nativity scene.

They have special services in church, sing carols, give presents and eat delicious food.

Id-ul-Fitr is a special time for Muslims. It marks the end of Ramadan. This is a month when Muslims fast during the day.

At Id, we wish each other 'Id Mubarak' which means 'Happy Id'.

There are all kinds of special times in people's everyday lives.

When a Muslim baby is born, its father whispers a prayer in its ear. Something sweet, like date juice, is placed on its tongue to bring a sweet and happy life.

In some Buddhist countries, boys become monks for a few months. At a joining ceremony, their heads are shaved and they are given monks' robes.

At a Sikh wedding, a hymn is sung as the couple walk around the Guru Granth Sahib.

People who do not follow a religion often share some of the same beliefs as religious people.

They believe in being kind, helping others and in treating people as they'd like to be treated themselves.

Everyone believes in something.
So, what do you believe?

Notes for teachers, parents and carers

Buddhism

Buddhists follow the teachings of a man called Siddhartha Gautama, who became the Buddha, or 'enlightened one'. He lived around 2,500 years ago. Buddhists use his teachings as a guide for their lives, and as a way of understanding how life truly is. Buddhism is unusual because, unlike many other religions, it is not based on a belief in a personal God who created and looks after the world. The Buddha did not claim to be a god and did not want to be worshipped as one.

Christianity

Christians believe in one God, and follow the teachings of Jesus, whom they call 'Christ'. They believe that Jesus was the Son of God, sent to Earth to save people from their sins. During his life, Jesus taught people about God's love for them. Christians believe that Jesus was crucified, but that he rose from the dead before ascending into Heaven to be with God. This is called the Resurrection, and shows that death is not the end but the start of a new life with God.

Hinduism

Hinduism is one of the oldest religions, with its roots in India more than 4,000 years ago. Today, there are around a billion Hindus. There are various ways of being a Hindu. Many Hindus believe in a great spirit, called Brahman, whom they sometimes call 'God'. They also worship gods and goddesses, who represent different aspects of Brahman's power. Hindus believe that every living thing has a soul (atman) which is reincarnated in another body when you die. This happens again and again until, by living a good life, you reach moksha, or freedom.

Humanism

Some people, such as Humanists, do not believe in God or in different gods, though they still have a set of beliefs to live their lives by. Humanists believe that people can live good lives without religious beliefs. They believe that we have only one life and that it is up to each person to create a good, meaningful life for themselves, and to make sense of the world around them, using reason and shared human values, such as right and wrong, living responsibly and caring for others.

Islam

Islam is a religion whose followers are called Muslims. The word 'Islam' means 'obedience' or 'submission' in Arabic. Muslims submit to the will of God, whom they called Allah, and follow Allah's guidance in their lives. Muslims believe that Allah sent messengers, called prophets, to teach people about Islam. The last and greatest of these was Muhammad who lived in Saudi Arabia around 1,400 years ago. Allah gave the Qur'an, the holy book of Islam, to Muhammad, so that Islam could never be changed again.

Judaism

Judaism is the religion of the Jewish people. It is one of the world's oldest religions, dating back some 4,000 years. Jews believe in one God who created the world. According to the Torah (the Jewish holy book), God chose a man called Abraham to be the father of the Jews. They believe that God made a covenant (agreement) with Abraham. God promised to guide and care for the Jews, if the Jews kept the laws that God had given to them and lived just and wise lives, loving God.

Sikhism

The Sikh religion began about 500 years ago in Punjab, India. At that time, the main religions of the region were Hinduism and Islam, but there were deep divisions between the two. Nanak, a holy man, introduced a new religion which promoted tolerance and equality. He became the first of ten Sikh gurus, or holy teachers. Sikhs believe in one God, and hope to grow closer to God through prayer and praise. Working hard, earning an honest living and looking after other people are also important aspects of being a Sikh.

Websites for Parents

www.bbc.co.uk/religion/religions/
Comprehensive information about a wide range of religions.

www.bbc.co.uk/programmes/articles/3lKZp31jBVJ2v3C2h1V03 kz/a-to-z-of-religion-and-beliefs
Introducing and exploring a variety of belief systems and related topics.

www.reonline.org.uk/
Providing ideas and resources to promote learning in RE.

www.humanism.org.uk/humanism/
Offering an extensive resources with a view to deepening public understanding of Humanism.

Useful words

elders   Older people who are important leaders and teachers of a religion.

equal   The same as.

fast   Go without food as part of worship in a religion.

holy   Linked to God and special to a religion.

incense   Sticks or cones that give off a sweet smell when burned.

offerings   Flowers, food, money and other objects offered to God or a god.

respect   A feeling of great admiration for a person.

worship   Show devotion, for example by saying prayers and singing songs.

Index